Back to the Basics
A training for Kingdom Workers

Adetokunbo Obasa

DEDICATION

To my wonderful wife Katherine and
my sons Joshua and Josiah. They have been
such a blessing to me.

CONTENTS

Acknowledgments i

1 Back to the Basics 1

2 Prayer 9

3 Fasting 13

4 Live for Christ 19

ACKNOWLEDGMENTS

I want to give thanks to God Almighty for His mercies and His blessings. My Sustainer, My Defender, My Helper, the One who has been so merciful to me. My appreciation goes to all the members of House of David (A Covenant Church), for their support and encouragement. My prayer is that the Lord will reward all your labors of love in Jesus Name. Amen.

My sincere appreciation goes to all my friends in the Ministry, men and women of God that the Lord has used to encourage us in obeying the Lord in the assignment He gave to us, may He send divine helpers to support your vision in Jesus Name. Amen.

I want to thank especially my covenant daughter, Julienne King for helping me. The Lord will bless you in Jesus Name. Amen.

I want to thank God for my Sweetheart, whom the Lord has used tremendously in my personal life and ministry. I cannot thank her enough, only God can reward her for all her labors in Jesus Name. Amen. The boys, I love them so much. My Father in Heaven who gave them to us will watch over them in Jesus Name. Amen.

BACK TO THE BASICS

God bless you. I want to use this extract from our worker's training in our ministry to encourage someone, a brother or a sister, in the Kingdom that needs encouragement and needs advice or counseling on how to get back to what they used to do for the Lord. I pray this will bless you as you read it in Jesus Name. Amen.

1 Samuel chapter 10 verse 27

But the children of Belial said, How shall this man save us? And they despised him and brought no presents. But he held his peace.

I pray for you today that you will honor God in your life. I want to talk briefly this morning about going back to the basics. Lamentations chapter 5 verse 21.

Turn thou us unto thee, O Lord, and we shall be turned; renew our days as of old.

Say, "turn me O' Lord". If you want God to do better in your life say turn me O'Lord. We need God to take us to another level. Do you want God to take you to another level? From a personal standpoint, I have so many desires in my heart and I want God to do more in my life than what I'm doing. As much as I hear Him and God gives me confidence and He keeps my soul at peace comforting me with words such an as, "My son I love you. I know that you have a hunger in your heart for me but there are seasons and time for everything." He encourages me to keep doing what I am doing and that I will get there. Sometimes we want to do more and go higher in the things of God. I know in my heart that as you are reading this, you want to pray better, read your Bible more, fast better and seek His will for your life.

Let's read Psalm 84 verse 7 (*They go from strength to strength, every one of them in Zion appeareth before God*). Every time you appear before him, you want to live differently. You want God to take you higher. You don't want to remain the same. I pray for you that you will leave every service and every program with a hunger in your spirit to want to do better for the Lord almighty. Every time you appear before him that He will take you to another level. Let's read psalm 42 verse 1, *(As the hart panteth after the water brooks, so panteth my soul after thee, O God)*. Is your soul panting after God? If your soul is panting after God shout hallelujah. When you are panting after God sincerely, he won't let you down. A hunger for his presence and not just to magnify your problems or issues, but to magnify Him, the Ancient of days, the Creator of all flesh, the Author of everything. Amen.

This training is meant to recharge your battery as a worker. You have laboured all year now you need to be recharged. Say, "Recharge me O'Lord." Most times when you get to the end that's when your battery wants to give up. That's when your battery will tell you I don't want to work anymore. I've been fasting all year, and nothing has happened. I've been praying and asking God for this in that and nothing has been done God has not moved on my case I have not seen the hand of God I have not seen the glory of God in my situation but as a worker when you are panting after God, you will be filled. There is no one in the word of God that panted after God sincerely that was not filled. No one that made room for God in their life was not attended to. God will attend to you. You don't climb a tree for nothing. Zacchaeus did not climb the tree for nothing. God will not allow it. Let's look at Daniel chapter one verse 8, God did not allow Daniel to propose in his heart "to not contaminate his soul with the Kings food" for nothing. God honored Daniel's position. Can you imagine a slave, a slave does not have options or even a name, saying that he doesn't want to eat certain foods, and God honored it. One man chose God over it all. There is no one that pants after God in want to take their relationship to another level that God did not honor. Even the 3 Hebrew boys in Daniel Chapter 11 That said that they will not bow down to the whims and caprices of the King. They said, "O'King, even if our God does not save us, we will not bow down." God still honored these boys. This is why I love Daniel 11:32, it reads *"And such as do wickedly against the covenant shall he corrupt by flatteries: but the people that do know their God shall be strong and do exploits".*

They that know their God… If you really know God, you will do exploits. God does not allow His knowledge of Him to be in vain. If you really know God and you stand up for Him, you will do exploits. Say, "I will stand up for God." When you stand up for God, sometimes you will be the only standing for the whole generation. You have to be strong. You can't shake because no one is on your side. When you really stand up for God, you will do exploits. So, we will be going back to the basics for this training. I want to share some things with you. Let's start with a Bible verse. Let's read Acts 2:41-42.

"Then they that gladly received his word were baptized: and the same day there were added unto them about three thousand souls. 42 And they continued stedfastly in the apostles' doctrine and fellowship, and in breaking of bread, and in prayers."

The first thing I want to talk to you about as a worker is going back to the Bible. Get back into your Bible, please. Get back into reading the Word of God. I beg you. If you really want to enjoy God, you must get back into reading your Bible. Give time to reading the Word of God. There is no time that I read the Word that I don't get shocked at what He reveals to me. I think, "how did I not see this before"? I say to myself that "I should have been quoting this verse in relationship to this verse so forth and so on". I say aloud to God, "Daddy, I didn't know that this was there." The only thing that He tells me is, "just read your Bible, you will see things." Any time you read it, you will discover new things, people of God. So, I'm begging you, get back to the Word. I don't know how you have been doing all of this time with your Bible reading, but I want to encourage you, get back into the Word of God. Let me give you a couple of Bible verses that will help you with the Word of God. God said something to someone in Joshua chapter 1 verses 7-9,

Only be thou strong and very courageous, that thou mayest observe to do according to all the law, which Moses my servant commanded thee: turn not from it to the right hand or to the left, that thou mayest prosper withersoever thou goest. 8 This book of the law shall not depart out of thy mouth; but thou shalt meditate therein day and night, that thou mayest observe to do according to all that is written therein: for then thou shalt make thy way prosperous, and then thou shalt have good success. 9 Have not I commanded thee? Be strong and of a good courage; be not afraid, neither be thou dismayed: for the Lord thy God is with thee whithersoever thou goest.

After all of the promises, God was telling this Prophet that "look what will keep you successful, what will bring you to this place of promise is the Word of God. Make sure that you do not depart from the Word, obey it, and be strong in your obedience." Now re-reading verse 8

This book of the law shall not depart out of thy mouth; but thou shalt meditate therein day and night, that thou mayest observe to do according to all that is written therein: for then thou shalt make thy way prosperous, and then thou shalt have good success.

"For then", I want you to pay attention to "for then". So that means that if you don't do this one, then the promise will not come to pass. No matter what the Lord has said, if you don't honor this Word, then you can forget it. You have to do this one in order to make His promises a reality. If you don't do this one, then you are not going anywhere. This is what the Body of Christ wants to do. We want to be successful, but we don't want to read the Bible. We want to have victories in life, but we don't want to read the Word of God. What is the Word of God? Let's read John 1:1-3.

In the beginning was the Word, and the Word was with God, and the Word was God. 2 The same was in the beginning with God. 3 All things were made by him; and without him was not anything made that was made.

Now, they are reverencing the Word as a human being, "was with Him". You should know that they are talking about Jesus. So, if they are talking about Jesus, that Jesus is the Word.

So, if you don't read your Bible, then there is no relationship with Jesus. Does that make sense? I'm saying this, for example, in math, $X + Y = Z$. Z exists because of $X + Y$. In mathematics, if the formula is wrong, your answer is wrong. Same way with our relationship with God. To get results from God, we must read the Word.

Let's read, Psalm 1 verses 1-3.

Blessed is the man that walketh not in the counsel of the ungodly, nor standeth in the way of sinners, nor sitteth in the seat of the scornful. 2 But his delight is in the law of the Lord; and in his law doth he meditate day and night. 3 And he shall be like a tree planted by the rivers of water, that bringeth forth his fruit in his season; his leaf also shall not wither; and whatsoever he doeth shall prosper.

The man is so prosperous because he is meditating on something day and night. I ask you, "what do you meditate on?" What is your driver? The Word of God is my driver. This is why I quote Bible off of my head because the Word of God is what drives me. When you see me do anything, it is because the Word of God is in my heart so strong. The Word of God makes me who I am. I am so in love with the Word of God that I take time to look into it. No matter how busy I am. As I was speaking to someone some time ago in my office, God was ministering to me about what to teach for this training. You must love Jesus that much, love Him enough to know about Him. How? By reading the Word. Anything you love,

7

you read about. Right? It's just a simple principle. Read your Bible.

Prayer Points

1. Thank Him for all that He has done for you.

2. Heavenly Father, I ask You to forgive me for not giving time to Your Word.

3. Heavenly Father, give me a hunger for Your Word.

4. Thank You for giving me the grace to study Your Word in Jesus Name. Amen.

PRAYER

You must pray. Any child of God that wants to succeed as a worker, must pray. You must be a prayer warrior. Jesus prayed. He prayed before He walked on top of the water. He prayed before He chose the disciples. He prayed on the mountain of transfiguration. It was in the place of prayer that Elias and Moses appeared to Him. He prayed in the garden of Gethsemane. If He had not prayed in the garden of Gethsemane, He would not have gone to that cross. Why, because the weight of our sins was so heavy. As a matter of fact, God has given some children of God a song, "Prayer is the key. Prayer is the key. Prayer is the master key. Jesus started with prayer. He ended with prayer. Prayer is the master key."

So, prayer is the key. It's the master key that opens all doors. If you don't know how to pray, ask God to give you help. Or contact me, I will give you personal lecture on prayer, but you must pray. Luke 18 verse 1 say

And he spake a parable unto them to this end, that men ought always to pray, and not to faint;

Let's look at 1 Thessalonians 5:17

Pray without ceasing.

The Bible gives an entire verse to it so that you can't miss it. *Pray without ceasing.* There are so many verses in the Bible about prayer. For example, Jeremiah 33:3

Call unto me, and I will answer thee, and show thee great and mighty things, which thou knowest not.

Prayer is essential. Prayer is essential for anything in life. Let's look at Daniel 9:1.

In the first year of Darius the son of Ahasuerus, of the seed of the Medes, which was made king over the realm of the Chaldeans;

Daniel came about a revelation and this is what he did. Let's read verse 2-3.

In the first year of his reign I Daniel understood by books the number of the years, whereof the word of the Lord came to Jeremiah the prophet, that he would accomplish seventy years in the desolations of Jerusalem. 3 And I set my face unto the Lord God, to seek by prayer and supplications, with fasting, and sackcloth, and ashes:

He came to a conclusion. If I want to change the situation, I must pray. If l want to change a situation, I must pray. If you want to change the story of your life, pray. Look at Daniel's prayer point in verse 4 of the same chapter

*And I prayed unto the LORD my God, and made my confession,
and said, O Lord, the great and dreadful God, keeping the covenant and
mercy to them that love him, and to them that keep his commandments;*

There is a process: (1) to them that love you (2) to them
that keep your commandments. God does not keep His
covenant with those that do not obey Him. If something is
going on in your life that you don't understand, check yourself.
Are you obeying God? Do you love Him? Do you care for
Him? Look at how Daniel started his prayer. He did not just go
to God asking for something. First of all, he honored God.
"Our Father, who art in Heaven. Hallowed by Thy Name".
First of all, honor God. Then Daniel went on in the next verse.
Let's look at verse 5 of the same chapter.

*We have sinned, and have committed iniquity, and have done
wickedly, and have rebelled, even by departing from thy precepts and from
thy judgments:*

Now, he came to his point. This is the reason that he is
praying. "Daddy, we have sinned." He didn't start with the
confession. He honored God. If you don't know how to pray
and you just begin in asking Him without greeting God,
"Daddy, how are you doing? Good morning", "You are a good
God", "You are a loving God", "Thank You for what You did
yesterday", "Thank You for what You did last year". You

didn't thank Him. You didn't say nothing, but just say I need Your help. I'm coming today because I need Your help. Is that the way to pray?

Prayer Points

1. Thank You Father for opening my eyes to the importance of prayer.

2. Heavenly Father, uproot in my life every spirit of prayerlessness in the Name of Jesus. Amen.

3. Heavenly Father, release upon fresh coals of fire for prayer in Jesus Name. Amen.

FASTING

Crucify your flesh. Any child of God that wants to be a good worker or want to serve God very well, you must crucify your flesh. If your flesh is your driver. You can't fast. You can't pray. Even Jesus Christ recommended fasting. Let's read Matthew 17:21.

Howbeit this kind goeth not out but by prayer and fasting.

If Jesus can recommend fasting and praying, then we need it. This is why it's good to read the Bible because there are recommendations there. "I don't know how to have victory in this area." "I don't know how to have joy in this area." "The enemy is coming to me in this area all the time." Then, go to the recommendation in the Bible. Go and search for a recommendation. This is why we need to read the Word. This is why I started with the Word. Then prayer. We have to read and pray. The next thing is to crucify your flesh because you have to do the first 2 things I said successfully, you have to crucify your flesh.

In order to crucify your flesh, you can just go before the Lord, "Lord, help me." The Lord will not help you. You have to discipline yourself. It's your choice. It's your decision. Either you are feeding your flesh or you are feeding your Spirit Man. You have to decide who is going to be in the driver seat. If you don't read your Bible all the time, guess what?, your flesh will be on the driver's seat. Because there is no Word that will help your spirit man to take charge.

He doesn't have any power to take charge because your flesh is what you are feeding all the time. So the flesh is in the driver's seat constantly. You want to come to church and your flesh will tell you no, why? Why must you come today. Pastor has not prayed for me. He's not looking at my situation. I'm still like this. So, why must I come. You will begin to feel like your coming to church is to help the Pastor. You don't see it as a duty. It's because you don't have the Word. If you have the Word in you, you will see coming to church as a duty.

No one will have to beg you to come to church. It's a duty. Does your manager come to your house and wake you up to report to work? If any company is doing that, let me know the company and I will go and work there. You know that your job is your duty and you will begin to look for a way to get to the job. You know your job description. You know your job schedule. When I was working at Continental and looking for people to work for me so that I could preach on Sundays, I never once called my manager saying, "please manager. You know that I am a Pastor. Can you please help me to find someone to work for me on Sunday shift?" I never did that for the first 7 years that I worked there. My manager does not know how I survived it. The only thing he knew is that I didn't work on Sundays. I didn't tell him to get people to come and work for me. That was my responsibility. So, let's read 1 Corinthians 9 verse 27.

But I keep under my body, and bring it into subjection: lest that by any means, when I have preached to others, I myself should be a castaway.

It is your responsibility that you are not going to give in to you, flesh. You must tell your flesh that it will not dictate to you what to do with your relationship and walk with God. One night I dealt with my flesh. I didn't leave church until about 9pm. At about 7pm, he was telling me that he was hungry. I told my flesh that this was not hunger unto death. Flesh, I am not leaving this place until I'm done. We have our prayer night so you need to calm down. Sometimes, your flesh talks to you.

You are so strong right? Your flesh doesn't talk to you. Alright, Pastor is faulty then. If you are so strong, we will see how far you will go. Does your flesh talk to you? My flesh said, Look'O, everyone has gone and you didn't eat. There's hot dog there. Go and get some hot dog for yourself. I said, "listen, I'm not eating until we do our prayer tonight." "So whatever you want to do, calm down."

You keep it in control. You are the one that keeps it.

Sometimes, I will tell you the truth, my flesh will tell me that I will fall down if I don't eat. I have to tell it, "you will not fall down". You determine what you will do. It's a determination to serve God. I have heard about all types of "fasting". "Water fasting". They will not eat but they carry a galloon of water with them. Their stomachs are not full of food, but it is full of water. You don't need food if your stomach is full of water. "Vegetable fasting". They will load up their plate with vegetables. That is not fasting. They are deceiving themselves. You keep your body. That is why I do dry fast. I recommend that because it keeps your body alert.

Let's go back to that verse, 1 Corinthians 9 verse 27.

But I keep under my body, and bring it into subjection: lest that by any means, when I have preached to others, I myself should be a castaway.

Your flesh can deceive you. It will say that where you are is so good. You don't need to change anything. You know God is merciful. Many times the enemy has come to me and said "look, nobody knows that you are fasting. Just break the fast now". "No one in the church knows that you are fasting. You are doing this for yourself. So nobody is in charge. Break it." I will say, no I will not. Those moments in my life is when I would face a major test after I decided not to break my fast.

After I have decided not to do it, sometimes that's the day that God would come through for me powerfully. Sometimes it is the day that I would receive an urgent call, saying "Pastor, I need your prayers now." I would say, "you see yourself devil. You wanted me to break that fast because you knew that this call was coming and I would be weak and wouldn't be able to pray."

So, it is you. If Brother Paul recommended that. He is the most senior Apostle in the Kingdom. If he says but "I keep. It is my responsibility". Then it is your responsibility as well to keep. God did not help Adam and advise Adam not to listen to his wife. God was waiting for Adam, "what are you going to do Adam?" It was his choice.

God was so close to Adam. God came down every evening and talk to Adam. "Adam, how was your day?" Asking Adam about the animals, if they are behaving. On the day that Adam ate the fruit, God did not show up. God waiting to see what he would do. It is your responsibility, people of God.

Proverbs 24 verse 10

If thou faint in the day of adversity, thou strength is small.

Prayer: Father, I come before you to ask for your mercy. Ancient of Days, I pray that all that I need to do to be a responsible worker, to do your will constantly, show it to me in Your Word. I heard Your message loud and clear. O'God, help me. In Jesus Name. Amen.

Final word/concluding thought: This is all the prayer you need. It's your choice now.

LIVE FOR CHRIST

If you are not on fire as you need to be, then you need to go back to the drawing board. It's very important. As a child of God, if you see yourself getting weary. Your zeal is no longer there, you need to check yourself. Something is missing. Most of the time, you just need to return back to the basics. Maybe you are not reading enough of the Bible. Maybe you are not praying enough anymore. Maybe you don't have time to spend with the Lord anymore. Those things you may not know that it is necessary, but you will just find out that your energy level for the things of God is reducing.

The devil is not concerned with your coming to Church. He is not concerned about you shouting Hallelujah and jumping. What he is concerned about is your daily activity with God. If he can get you to begin to draw back in those things that guides you spiritually, he has gotten you. You will not even know that you are drawing back. You will not even know that you are not doing what you are supposed to be doing. You will say that I am busy. You will just assume that you are ok. You will see that your spiritual man will be prompting you, and then your spiritual man will just stop.

This is because you have been so drawn into your
schedule, so much so that you don't even check yourself
anymore. You get home and do everything you have to do.
You go to bed. Wake up and start again. The enemy is so
crafty. He will keep you busy. Like Martha. Martha was busy
with everything, but she left what was important. We can be
running around for God and doing all these things for people,
helping, but the purpose for your existence, you have left that
one alone. The enemy is so crafty. You will begin to justify
yourself. "At least I am helping. At least I am doing
something."

Those things are good. Martha told Jesus Christ, "will you
tell my sister to come and help me. I am busy trying to do
ministry." Jesus told her, "Yes, what you are doing is good, but
Mary has chosen the better part." There's a better part. If the
Holy Spirit does not tell you. You may not even know. What
you are doing, you will think that you are on the right path.
There is a better part. It is that better part that will sustain you.
It is that part that you are leaving undone that will give you
strength towards the end. It is that better part that will make
you finish strong. That will make you finish well.

Whether we like it not, Jesus is coming back and your
position as a worker matter. As a worker, we have to remain
focused and grounded. We cannot lose any ground to the

enemy. He is still at work full time. If you noticed, the enemy didn't attack Jesus during the fasting. He waited until Jesus was very tired and weak. "Turn this stone to bread." We must be at alert and watching on the wall as members are relaxing. As a worker you must fast. If you don't fast, who is going to watch out for others?

Someone must watch out, right? That's why soldiers don't have breaks. You notice officers don't have breaks. Someone must be watching America. The Bible tells me and you that we are soldiers. Even though the Body of Christ has become so complacent, many members of the Body of Christ do not see themselves as soldiers. They see only the Pastors, workers, head of departments as soldiers. They believe that the fasting and prayers only belong to the workers and the ministers.

They don't feel like that they have to do all that. Actually, people of God, that is a wrong perception in the Body of Christ today. That's why many in the Body of Christ are so laid back today. They lean on the workers, ministers, and Pastors to carry them along. How can you carry a 20 year old baby? That's why the church is so bogged down with weight. Pastors are still carrying members that have been in the Church for years on their head. Still telling them little things that they should have matured to do by themselves. That is why the Pastors are wearing out. That's what is happening people of

God. I'm just trying to analyze the spiritual position of the Church so, you will understand why we are the way we are.

If it was not the mercy of God that has kept you and I with what is going on in the Body of Christ. Many churches would have shut down, if not for someone interceding or always on the wall praying constantly. Let us pray that the work of God in our hands will not be put to shame.

The things of the spiritual cannot be done by power. If it is by power, they would not be questioning Samson's strength. Samson was a small man. If he was a man with muscles, they would not want to find out why is he so strong. It is because Samson was a small man and they saw what he was doing. They were wondering how can a small man do this? It's very essential that we remain constantly on the wall seeking the face of God. Praying. People of God, sometimes it's tough. I'm not going to stand here as if it's so easy to pray. One hour of prayer equals to 8 hours on a job.

The energy that you use to pray for one hour is equal to an 8-hour job because of what comes out of you spiritually. This is the minimum of what Jesus required of His disciples. When He was in the garden of Gethsemane, He asked His disciples to watch with Him for one hour. He told the disciples, "Can you not watch with me for one hour?" That is the minimum that Jesus requires from any worker. That's why when I go into prayer, I don't pray less than one hour. This is the standard of Jesus. As a worker, in the Kingdom, it is very important.

Let's look at Lamentation 5 verse 21

Turn thou us unto thee, O Lord, and we shall be turned;
renew our days as of old.

There is an old part that is better than the new. Yes, we talk about the new testament a lot, but to tell the truth, if there was no old testament, there is no new testament. As a matter of fact, the plan for salvation started from the old testament. So, if there was no old testament, there cannot be anything new. Matter of fact, the old blessing is what Jesus came to connect us to- the blessings of Abraham from Genesis Chapter 12.

Jesus Christ did not come to bless us again, but to give you and I spiritual authority to be able to operate in the level of Abraham's blessing. It's very important that as a leader or a worker to go back to the Word. Read your Bible. If your Bible is not your friend, if your spirit is rejecting Bible study, then you need to check yourself because Jesus is the Word. You need to ask the Lord to come and be your savior again. There is no law against that. You can ask as many times as you want. Submit your life to Him again.

You must pray. Prayer is like a food. Prayer is the master key. Jesus started with prayer and ended with prayer. Prayer is the master key that opens all doors. As a child of God, you don't like prayer, you don't like to talk to God, you don't even like to say good morning to God, you can't talk to your father before you leave your house. You leave out again, come back home, there is no good afternoon, no good evening.

Even when we just go to the store and come back in, we thank God when we get back into the house. You know why? Many people have left out and they didn't make it back. Just as I was leaving one morning for church and I just wanted to watch the news before I left out. A woman just pulled over on the shoulder of I10 and an 18-wheeler came and struck her where she was and the woman died. So, you go out and come back in and you think that it is a normal day. You just think that it is normal for you to do that. The woman just stopped.

We don't know if she was talking to somebody. She just pulled over. Sometimes here in this country, if the call is important, some people will just pull over. Only God knows why this woman pulled over and she got hit. The woman died on the spot. So you go out and you come back in, you cannot be humble enough to thank God for bringing you back home?

You can't just come into your house and go about as if it

was not important. Many have gone out like you and they didn't come back. So, I make it a point of duty in my house to do that. When we go out and come back in, we thank God. Before we go to bed, we pray. It just lets God know that you appreciate every moment of your life. As a worker, you must be able to do that. I'm talking about prayer.

It is your responsibility to crucify the flesh. We have talked extensively about crucifying the flesh. We must be matured enough to discipline our flesh. If you love everybody that loves you, there is no reward for that. Jesus said that in Matthew Ch.5 verse 20, "except your righteousness exceeds that of the Saduccess and the Pharisees, you will not enter the Kingdom of Heaven." So, if you love people that love you back, there's no reward for that. So, I don't understand why in the church, people cannot talk to each other. In the church, you cannot relate to each other, and you are in this building. What kind of Christian are you? You must be matured enough to love everyone with the love of Christ.

I have a lot of friends. Does everyone do what I like? No. I still love them because I love them above their faults. If I want to pick a fault, I can pick fault in everyone. If I want to fight with someone, I can pick fault. So, if you are looking for faults, you cannot survive as a child of God and as a worker. You need people around you to do the work. You cannot be picking fault because you too are smelling somewhere. Say, "I am smelling somewhere." We are all smelling somewhere. God is just merciful in that we are all covered. Right? No matter how good you may think you look, we are all smelling somewhere. We can't follow you to the restroom. There is no one that loves you enough to come and sit with you in the rest room while you do number 2. You cannot point fingers.

The Bible clearly states in Matthew 7:1.

Judge not, that ye be not judged.

The Bible gives a verse to it. Don't point fingers at other people's lives so that people will not judge you as well. Stop picking at people. You cannot be everybody's friend, and everybody cannot be your friend. Do what you have to do. Relate with one another. Everyone will not be coming to your house to sit and eat dinner with you. You don't have to do that, but there is a level of relationship.

You can relate with people on your job. You talk to them, but do you go to their houses because you talk to them? You relate. That is a standard courtesy for every human being. Talk to somebody, but in the church, it is even better. It should be better. They don't have to come to your house for you to love them. They don't have to stay around you before you love them. You should be able to love anyway. We are serving the same God, so you should be matured enough to receive correction. Hebrews 12 verse 7.

> *If ye endure chastening, God dealeth with you as with sons;*
> *for what son is he whom the father chasteneth not?*

If you are truly a child of God, you should be able to receive correction. If God does not correct you, you need to check yourself. If God does not correct you anymore and everything you do is so correct, good, nobody talks to you to tell that you that you are wrong, you need to check yourself'O.

Hebrews 12 verse 8

> *But if ye be without chastisement, whereof all are partakers,*
> *then are ye bastards, and not sons.*

God says, "if I have not corrected you in months, then you are not my son or I'm not related to you." "I don't have any relationship with you." This is the Word of God. I didn't write it there. It says, "therefore, are ye, bastards". If God does not correct you, everything you do is correct. Some people just cannot take correction. They say, "you are judging me". No, we are not judging you, we are correcting you. There is a difference unless you have condemned yourself. That's why you feel condemned. This is a correction. If God does not correct you, then something is wrong. You are not a perfect human being. You make mistakes, and if someone says anything to you about it, then you build up your wall of defense. You are full of pride. You say, "no one can say anything to me. I'm doing the best I can." On who's score sheet is that? Is it your score sheet or God's score sheet? You are scoring yourself. Who is scoring who? Are you scoring yourself or God?

Have you thought about what God thinks about what you are doing? Have you asked Him? Did He give you a score mark? Did He give you 80% for your attitude or your behavior? Let Him be the One to score you not you scoring yourself. You cannot be the one that score yourself. Let God score you and see what you are going to get. So, the Lord said "if I don't correct you anymore, you are not my son." "You are not related. You are a bastard." Hebrews 12 verse 8

But if ye be without chastisement, whereof all are partakers, then are ye bastards, and not sons.

I have seen people walk away from the Church because you have corrected them. I don't think people are reading their Bible enough because if they had been reading before, they would just be humble. Hebrews 12 verse 9

Furthermore we have had fathers of our flesh which corrected us, and we gave them reverence: shall we not much rather be in subjection unto the

Father of spirits, and live?

So when God corrects you, it is for your profit. He is trying to help you. The reason for the correction is that He is trying to allow you to enjoy some things. We can't because we have built up our wall of defenses, "nobody can talk to me", "I'm doing the best I can". Hebrews 12 verse 10

For they verily for a few days chastened us after their own pleasure; but he for our profit, that we might be partakers of his holiness.

God knows it's not going to feel good in your flesh. He knows that, but look at what He says.

11 Now no chastening for the present seemeth to be joyous, but grievous: nevertheless afterward it yieldeth the peaceable fruit of righteousness unto them which are exercised thereby.

Say "afterward". That means that those people that accept the correction, that sit down and thank God for using His servant to correct you, afterward, if you are patient, it will yield peaceable fruit. Many people are not patient enough to see the result. So, after you correct them, they are grievous and there are sympathizers in the Church who will go behind the Pastor and say, "sorry for the way Pastor talk to you. Me too, I didn't like it either and I wouldn't take it." They come and spoil your destiny and come begging you. They will not allow this process to be completed. They will interrupt it here in the place of pain and support you physically and use their hand to rub your head and having you like a baby. You will remain a baby and not allow God to complete what He wants to do in your life. Many are like that today.

As a child of God, as a worker, you must make up your mind that you want to live for Christ. If you have not made up your mind, then you are not ready. As a worker, as a worker in the Church, now, it's not about titles. This is why I don't like titles. Don't get me wrong, I have a title, I'm a Pastor. What I meant is that, I don't like all these kinds of title, apostle, bishop, because all of these titles comes with a sacrifice.

Apostles comes with a sacrifice. You die on the job. Bishops, you are a servant. You don't wear regalia and everyone is running after you, no, you serve. You labor. Your assignment is that you are groaning for people asking God for knowledge everyday so that you can impact destinies. God calls Bishops to teach. Pastors are called to nurture the body, to be given a Word that will suit the soul that will challenge him/her to do more for the Lord. To be given an understanding in the Word. This is the assignment for a Pastor. That's why Jeremiah 3 verse 15 says...

And I will give you pastors according to mine heart,
which shall feed you with knowledge and understanding.

This is why a Pastor cannot give old manna. You cannot give old food or stale food. A Pastor has to feed the people with knowledge and understanding. So, if a Pastor is not getting fresh manna from the Lord, the people will be eating stale food. They will not have any understanding. They will not have any knowledge, and they will be crippled on the journey of salvation. When you don't have knowledge and understanding, you are crippled.

That's what Hosea 4 verse 6 says

My people are destroyed for lack of knowledge: because thou hast rejected
knowledge, I will also reject thee, that thou shalt be no priest to me: seeing
thou hast forgotten the law of thy God, I will also forget thy children.

So, lack of knowledge can kill people. Not witches or wizards or devil. Forget devil. Lack of understanding and knowledge can destroy destinies. You will not have what you are supposed to have, but because you have no understanding of how to use it or apply it, you perish.

Proverbs 4 verse 7 says something

Wisdom is the principal thing; therefore get wisdom:
and with all thy getting get understanding.

This wisdom is the other part of knowledge. Knowledge plus understanding is very crucial to any child of God. Wisdom and understanding. You must live for Christ. You must settle it in your spirit.

John 6 verse 38

> *For I came down from heaven, not to do mine own will,*
> *but the will of him that sent me.*

This must get into your spirit. Once you get it into your spirit, they will not beg you to serve God again. They will not beg you to give to the ministry. They will not beg you to support the work. They will not beg you because you know the reason of your existence is because of Him. You came down to do His will.

You did not come down to your local church on your own. You came down to your local church because He decided that your local church is your house. And, if He located you there, then you must make sure that you must do the will of Him who sent you here. That's how you are going to succeed in life. That's how you are going to make it in life, when you do the will of Him that has sent you. Everything that He has asked you to do, you must do with joy. You live for Him.

Let's read Galatians 2 verse 20

I am crucified with Christ: nevertheless I live; yet not I, but Christ liveth
in me: and the life which I now live in the flesh I live by the faith of the
Son of God, who loved me, and gave himself for me.

This man has removed himself from the equation. He says that
"I am alive, but it is Christ that lives in me." You must settle
this verse in your spirit that you are alive. You were once dead,
but now you are alive in Christ. And, it is this Christ that you
are living for. You don't have any other plan.

Everything that you have, belongs to Him. You have no
plan. Your time belongs to Him. You are completely sold out.
As a matter of fact, once we don't have anything to do in the
Church, I don't know what to do with myself. Christ is your
life. Now, some of you are not called to be a Pastor and you
cannot be like me, but you even on your job, your home,
everything you do, Christ must be seen. People around you
must see Christ in you.

Your children should not just fear you. You should not
come into the house and your children run into the restroom
to hide from you because you are like "Margaret Thatcher".
Shouting and screaming. They don't see your teeth outside. No
joy. No smile. They will wonder what kind of God are we
serving in our house? This is why some of these children, when
they grow up like this, they go to universities and they never

come back. They don't like our God because of the way God has been projected to them over these years. They conclude that if God is like this, then they don't want to serve our God. You don't smile. You don't crack jokes. You are so serious. No smile at all. Just commands. No time for recreation. No laughter in the house.

They will wonder what kind of God are we serving. Is this God this mean? Is He a mean God? God is not that mean. God cracks jokes. He has made me laugh several times. I'm alone in the car, driving along, and He shows me something and I just laugh. Even in the face of the enemy, God laughs. Is that not what it says in the Bible?

Let's read together Psalm 2 verse 1-4

Why do the heathen rage, and the people imagine a vain thing? 2 The kings of the earth set themselves, and the rulers take counsel together, against the LORD, and against his anointed, saying, 3 Let us break their bands asunder, and cast away their cords from us. 4 He that sitteth in the heavens shall laugh: the LORD shall have them in derision.

If God is laughing, why can't you smile? Huh, look at God. After they have gathered themselves together, He laughs. In the face of war, God was laughing. Here we are praying in tongues and God is asking why are we stressing ourselves. He's laughing, saying that "they are not fighting against you alone. I am there with you". In the face of serious warfare, God is laughing and we in our house, no laughter. There is no problem, but still don't laugh. So, when there is problem, what will you do? Live for Christ, people of God. Let Christ be real to everybody around you. Let Christ be real.

Matthew 5 verse 16

> *Let your light so shine before men, that they may see your good works, and glorify your Father which is in heaven.*

James 1 verses 23-25

> [23] *For if any be a hearer of the word, and not a doer, he is like unto a man beholding his natural face in a glass:* [24] *For he beholdeth himself, and goeth his way, and straightway forgetteth what manner of man he was.* [25] *But whoso looketh into the perfect law of liberty, and continueth therein, he being not a forgetful hearer, but a doer of the work, this man shall be blessed in his deed.*

I love that. That's I said let's read it. This is a good Word. So, if you are not just reading the Word of God, but you are applying it daily, you will be a blessed man. The last point is that we must be a soul winner. As a worker in the Church, we must win souls. Not only win souls for Christ, because you are an instrument in His hands and an extension of His, but also endeavor for God to use you to populate the church. It must be one of your assignments for the coming year to invite your friends. You know what God has done in your life here. Some of your friends are sitting in wrong places because of comfort. It's comfortable for them. Their friends are there. They are not getting any spiritual growth or nourishment. They are just sitting there because their friends go there. You would be surprised as to why people go to their church.

I have one member of the Church that God ministered to me that he should be coming to this ministry and be a minister. Each time I told him, he would say let me pray about it. This was over a space of 2 years. One day I called him for something or another and reminded him of what the Lord said.

He told me that he has been praying about it because he said that when he comes, he wants to stay. He doesn't want it to be that when he is corrected, he will leave. So he is praying that whatever I would tell him, won't hurt his feelings. He wants to come to stay. My prayer was that the Lord would speak to him quickly and the Lord did. He has come and since then with his family and he doesn't play with the work. He knows who brought him here. Everyone has come into the ministry for a reason. So, do the work. Be a doer of the work so that you can be blessed. He and his family has been blessed since he has obeyed God. To let him know that He was the one that sent him to the ministry, he has been blessed.

Once you are a doer of the work, you will be blessed. So, you must win souls. Proverbs 11 verse 30

> The fruit of the righteous is a tree of life;
> and he that winneth souls is wise.

You know what God is doing in your life, so bring somebody along. So that those people can be blessed and enjoy what you have enjoyed. I pray that the Lord, God Almighty will help us in the mighty Name of Jesus. Amen.

Prayer Points

1. Father, I thank You for taking me back to my first love.

2. Heavenly Father, forgive me in any way that I have not represented You well.

3. Heavenly Father, give me the grace to be an extension of You in this end time, in the Name of Jesus. Amen.

ABOUT THE AUTHOR

Adetokunbo Obasa is another fellow laborer in the vineyard of our Lord and Savior, Jesus Christ, through the power of the Holy Ghost. The Pastor of House of David, A Covenant Church, located in Houston, Texas is grounded as a ministry where the power of God dwells, the grace of God abounds, the mercy of God is received and everyone is Heaven bound. Amen.

Made in the USA
Middletown, DE
09 January 2022

58227543R00028